4/10

Frankford Public Library
8 Main Street
Frankford, DE 19945
(302) 732-9351

DAILY OVERDUE FINE....... 10 cents

D1269483

Animal Camouflage in the Forest

Hidden in Nature

by Martha E. H. Rustad

Consulting editor: Gail Saunders-Smith, PhD
Consultant: Tanya Dewey, PhD
University of Michigan Museum of Zoology

Capstone
press ®

Mankato, Minnesota

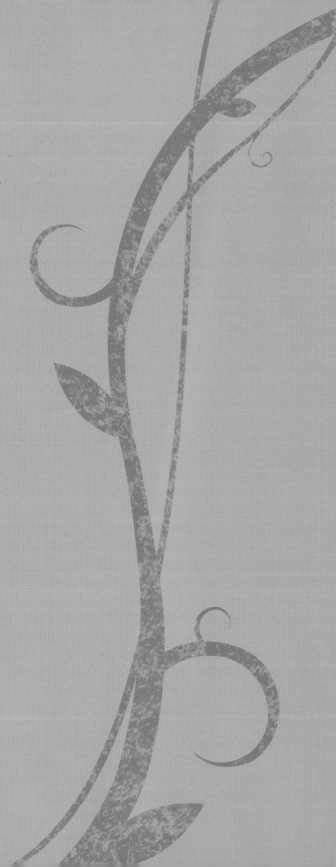

Pebble Plus is published by Capstone Press,
151 Good Counsel Drive, P.O. Box 669, Mankato, Minnesota 56002.
www.capstonepress.com

Copyright © 2010 by Capstone Press, a Capstone Publishers company. All rights reserved.
No part of this publication may be reproduced in whole or in part, or stored in a retrieval system, or transmitted in any form or by any means, electronic, mechanical, photocopying, recording, or otherwise, without written permission of the publisher. For information regarding permission, write to Capstone Press,
151 Good Counsel Drive, P.O. Box 669, Dept. R, Mankato, Minnesota 56002.
Printed in the United States of America

 Books published by Capstone Press are manufactured with paper containing at least 10 percent post-consumer waste.

Library of Congress Cataloging-in-Publication Data
Rustad, Martha E. H. (Martha Elizabeth Hillman), 1975–
    Animal camouflage in the forest / Martha E.H. Rustad.
    p. cm. — (Pebble Plus. Hidden in nature)
    Includes bibliographical references and index.
    Summary: "Simple text and photographs present animals that are camouflaged in the forest" — Provided by publisher.
    ISBN 978-1-4296-3324-6 (library binding)
    1. Forest animals — Juvenile literature. 2. Camouflage (Biology) — Juvenile literature. I. Title. II. Series.
QL112.R865 2010
591.47'2 — dc22   2009007304

Editorial Credits
Erika L. Shores, editor; Abbey Fitzgerald, designer; Svetlana Zhurkin, media researcher

Photo Credits
Getty Images/National Geographic/Tim Laman, 13
iStockphoto/Dieter Spears, 5; Jennifer Foeller, cover
Minden Pictures/Michael & Patricia Fogden, 21; Piotr Naskrecki, 11; Rachel Hingley, 19
Peter Arnold/Ed Reschke, 9
Photoshot/Bruce Coleman/Jen & Des Bartlett, 15
Shutterstock/Bill Sarver, 1; Rob Huntley, 17; Tony Campbell, 7

Note to Parents and Teachers

The Hidden in Nature set supports national science standards related to life science. This book describes and illustrates animal camouflage in the forest. The images support early readers in understanding the text. The repetition of words and phrases helps early readers learn new words. This book also introduces early readers to subject-specific vocabulary words, which are defined in the Glossary section. Early readers may need assistance to read some words and to use the Table of Contents, Glossary, Read More, Internet Sites, and Index sections of the book.

Table of Contents

In the Forest

In a leafy world,

animals need to blend in.

Camouflage in the forest

helps animals stay safe.

Squirrels in the forest
blend in with tree bark.
These furry animals stay still
when they hear predators.

Gray tree frogs have spots

that match tree trunks.

These frogs can change color

to match their surroundings.

Horned leaf chameleons

stay safe on the forest floor.

They look like dead leaves.

Predators can't spot them.

Birds in the Forest

Black and brown feathers hide

screech owls in hollow trunks.

Owls rest during the day.

They hunt at night.

Frogmouth birds have
black and white feathers.
These birds look like
tree branches.

Bugs in the Forest

A green body hides

a katydid in the forest.

Its body looks like a leaf.

Peppered moths match
tree bark.
They hide from birds
during the day.

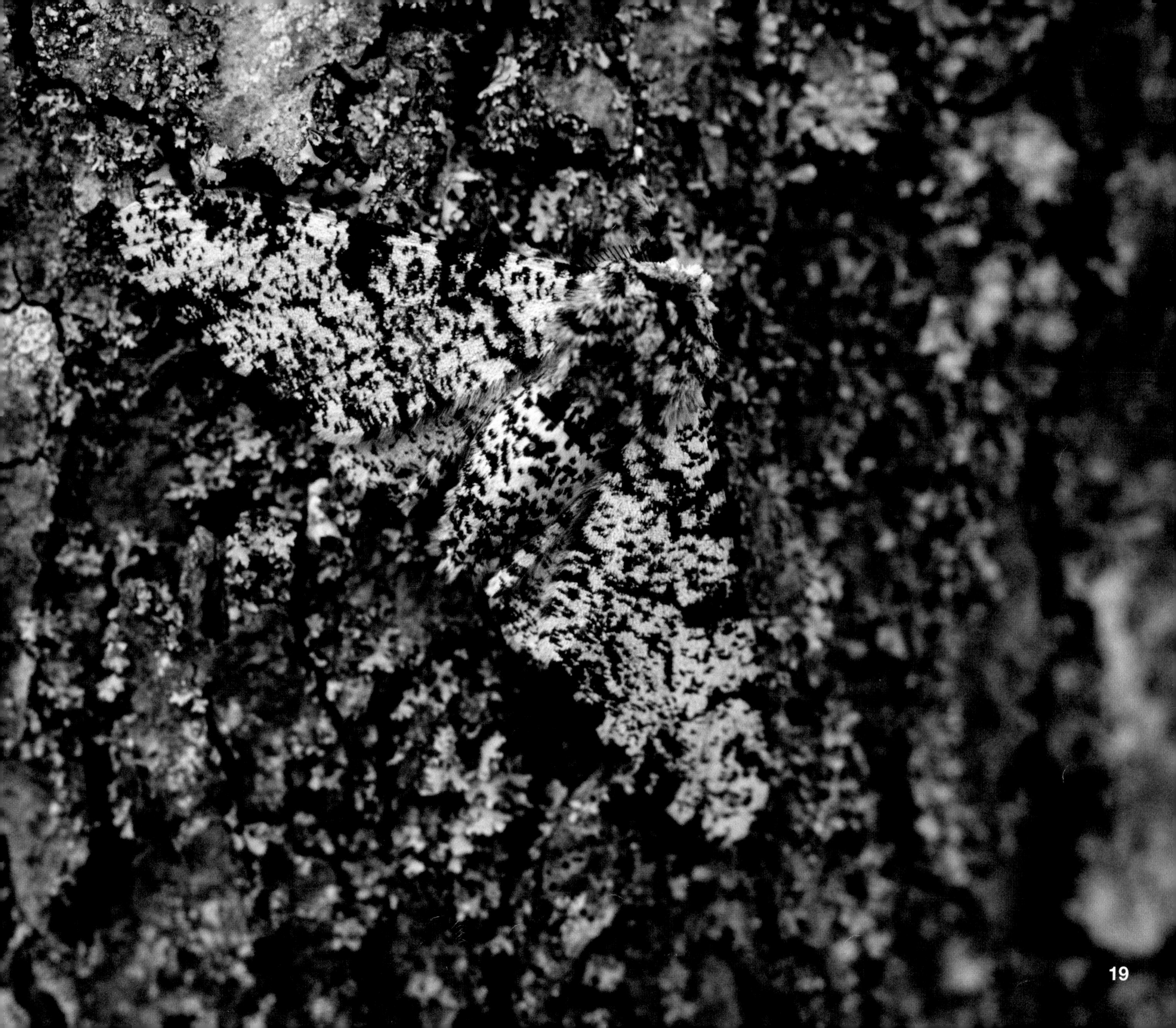

The white spots of bird-dropping

spiders hide them on leaves.

Birds won't eat anything

that looks like droppings.

Glossary

camouflage — coloring or covering that makes animals look like their surroundings

hollow — empty on the inside

katydid — a large, green insect that is like a grasshopper; male katydids rub their front wings together to make a noise that sounds like "katydid."

predator — an animal that hunts other animals for food

Read More

Helman, Andrea. *Hide and Seek: Nature's Best Vanishing Acts.* New York: Walker & Co., 2008.

Mitchell, Susan K. *Animals with Crafty Camouflage: Hiding in Plain Sight.* Amazing Animal Defenses. Berkeley Heights, N.J.: Enslow, 2009.

Internet Sites

FactHound offers a safe, fun way to find Internet sites related to this book. All the sites on FactHound have been researched by our staff.

Here's all you do:

Visit *www.facthound.com*

FactHound will fetch the best sites for you!

Index

Word Count: 148
Grade: 1
Early-Intervention Level: 18